Endangered Animals Of North America

Big Print
Colouring Book

This book belongs to:

The Canada Lynx
From: Northern
Canada

The Moose
From: Nova Scotia,
Canada

The Polar Bear
From: Alaska & Canada

Wolverine
From: Labrador, Quebec
Canada

The Baja Pronghorn
From: California

The California Condor
From: USA & Mexico

The Black Footed Ferret
From: Eastern North America

The American Bison
From: Canada, United States
& Mexico

The Beluga Whale
From: Canada

The Steller sea lions
From:Alaska to
California, USA

The Vancouver Marmot
From: British Columbia,
Canada

The Oahu Tree Snail
From: Hawaii, USA

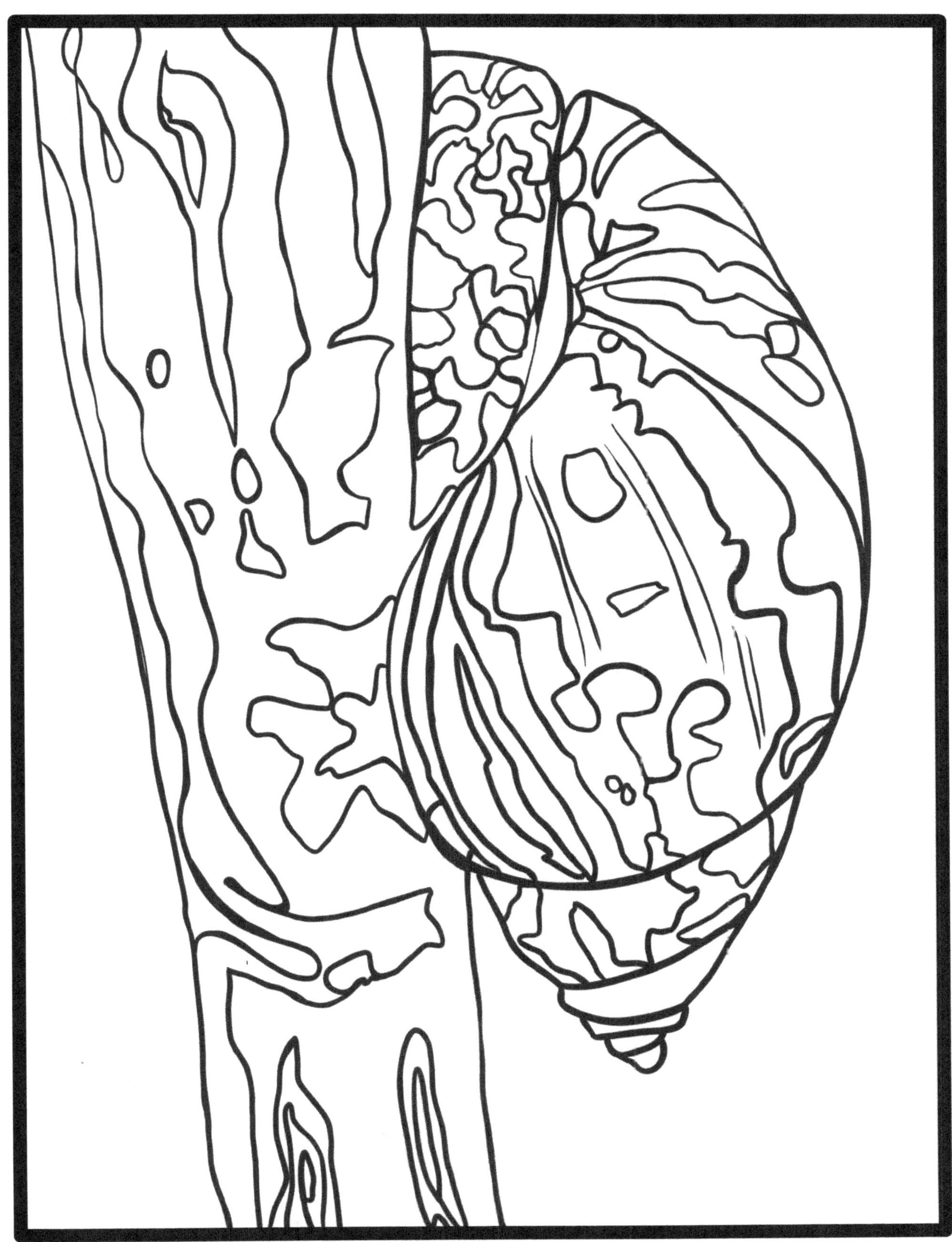

The Red Wolf
From: North Carolina,
Tennessee,&Texas

The Narwhal
From: Arctic, Canada

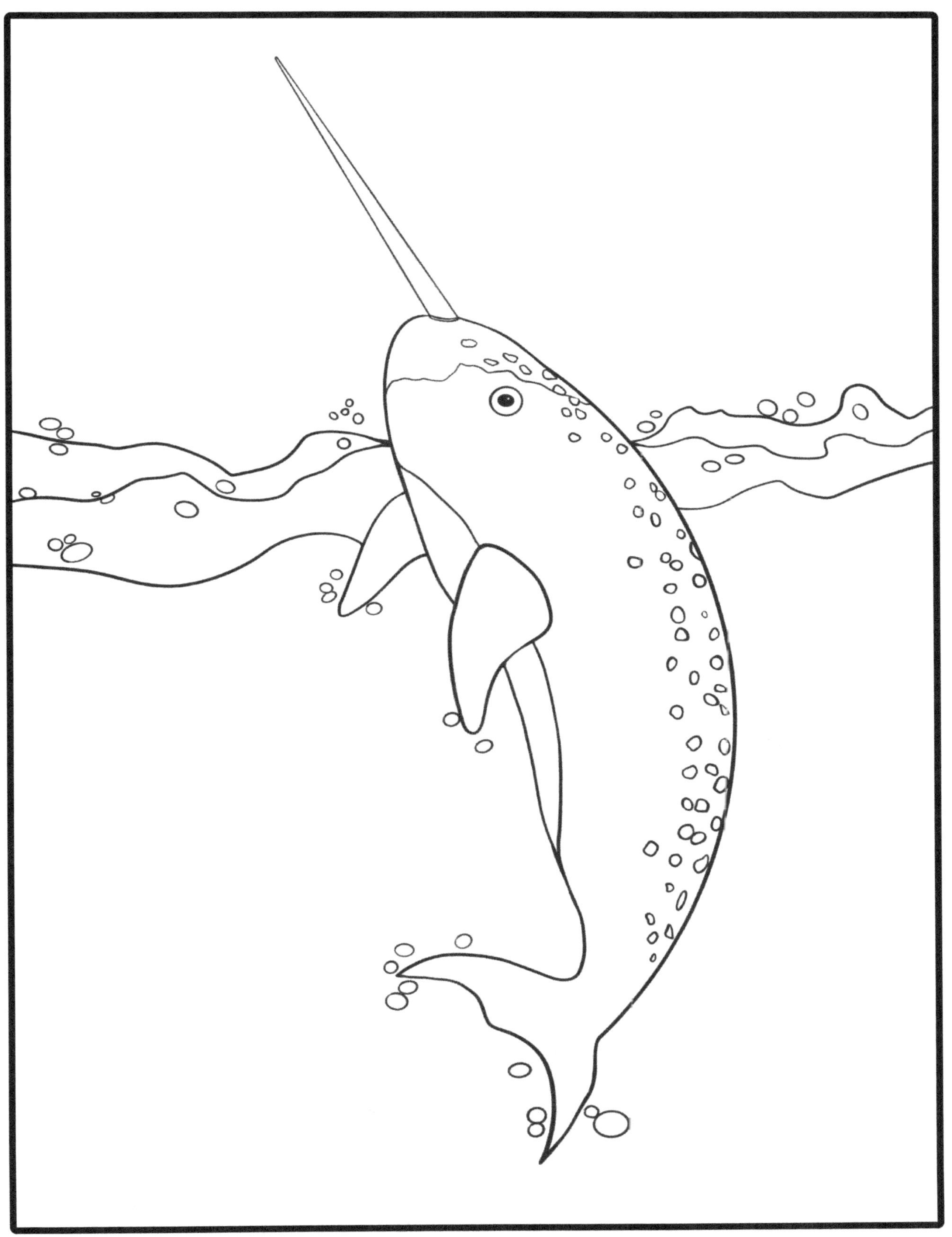

The Grizzly Bear
From: Canadian Arctic,
 Canada

The Burrowing Owl
From: Western Canada

The Greater Prairie Chicken.
From: Grasslands National Park,
Saskachewan, Canada

The American Badger,
From: North America (all over)

The Sea Otter
From: British Columbia,
 Canada

The Gray Wolf
From: Yellowstone, USA

The Panther
From: Florida to Mississippi
to Arkansas

The Mountain Goat
From: Western Canada

The Columbia Basin Pygmy Rabbit
From: Washington State, USA

The Gila Monster
From: Southern USA

The Texas Ocelot,
From: USA

The Peninsular Bighorn Sheep
California, USA

The Peary Cariboo,
From: Nova Scotia, Prince
Edward Island &
New Brunswick

The Peregrine Falcon
From: All over Canada

The Canadian Warbler
From: All over Canada

The Monarch Butterfly
East of Rocky Mountains, N.A.

Look for my next colouring book: Endangered animals of the world